The Cats of France

True Stories, Forgotten History, and Curious Trivia About French Cats

Séamus Mullarkey

The Cats of France

Copyright ©2025 Séamus Mullarkey

All rights reserved. No part of this publication may be reproduced, distributed, or transmitted in any form or by any means, including photocopying, recording, or other electronic or mechanical methods, without the prior written permission of the publisher, except in the case of brief quotations embodied in critical reviews and certain other non-commercial uses permitted by copyright law.

Plain Scribes Press

Paperback: 978-1-960227-69-0

Hardcover: 978-1-960227-68-3

DON'T MISS THIS SPECIAL BONUS

GET YOUR *FREE BOOK* TODAY

IT'S SO SIMPLE – AND TOTALLY FREE! – SCAN THE CODE OR CLICK THE LINK....

subscribepage.io/7565d5

Table of Contents

INTRODUCTION 8
LA LUXE - FASHION & LUXURY 10
   The King Who Built French Fashion 11
   Choupette Le Chat 11
   Purr-fectly Chic: Louis Vuitton's Catogram Collection 13
CATS IN FRENCH HISTORY 14
   Cattus Romanus - The Latin legacy 15
   Cats at the Royal French Court 15
LA CUISINE - MICHELIN STAR KITTIES IN THE KITCHEN .. 19
LA GUERRE - MILITARY KITTIES 22
   World War I 23
   World War II 24
PAYSAGES ET MONUMENTS - LANDSCAPES AND
LANDMARKS 26
   Catwalks of the Middle Ages: Strolling Down Ruelle des Chats 27
   Graveyard Gardens & Graffiti 27
   Feline Street Art 28
LES RACES FÉLINES - CAT BREEDS 29
   Chartreux: The uniquely French breed 30
   Serrade Petit 31
   Birman - mythical origins in Burma but modern origins in France 32
INSTITUTIONS FRANÇAISES - FRENCH INSTITUTIONS 33
   Les Chats du Ministère: When French Bureaucracy Meets Feline
   Flair 34
   Hospitals and Nursing Homes 34
LES GRANDS AMANTS DU CHAT - MAJOR FRENCH CAT
LOVERS 35
   Joachim Du Bellay and his lament for his cat 36

 Michel de Montaigne 36
 Madame Dupuis 37
 Moncrif's Les Chats 38
 Alexandre Dumas 39
 Victor Hugo 39
 Théophile Gautier 40
 Charles Baudelaire 41
 Pierre Loti 42
 Colette 43
 Jean Cocteau 44
 Charles de Gaulle 44

LES ENNEMIS DU CHAT - BOO, HISS! 46

LES CHAT DANS LES TRADITIONS POPULAIRES - THE CAT IN FRENCH FOLKLORE 48

 The Black Cat Cure 48
 The Matagot 49
 The White Cat Princess 50
 La Fontaine's Raminagrobis, Raton, and Rodilard 50
 Charles Perrault's Puss in Boots 51

LES CHAT DANS LA LANGUE FRANÇAISE - CATS IN THE FRENCH LANGUAGE 53

 French Nursery Rhymes 54
 French Proverbs 55
 Kitty Idioms and Expressions 56
 What French cats say 57

LE JEU DES NOMS - THE NAME GAME 58

LES CAFÉS - FOR PEOPLE, AND FOR CATS! 60

PHILOSOPHES ET INTELLECTUELS - PHILOSOPHERS AND INTELLECTUALS 63

 Jean-Jacques Rousseau 64
 Jacques Derrida 64

LA MUSIQUE - MUSIC AND THE PURR-FORMING ARTS ... 66

 Feline Melodies 67

LE CINEMA - FRENCH FELINE MOVIE STARS 68

    Film Pioneers with Paws 69
    Gay Purr-ee 69
    Le Chat 70
    A Musical Cat Lover 70
    A Cat in Paris 71

LE SCIENCE -SCIENTIFIC KITTIES 72
    Solid or Liquid? 73
    A Cat's Fall 73
    Cats and Communication 74

LES GRANDES ODYSSÉES FELINES -FELINE EXPLORERS AND ADVENTURERS 75
    Félicette, the first (and only) cat in space 76
    Misele 77
    Cocci 77
    The Hatching Cat 78

LES CHATS DANS LES ARTS VISUELS -CATS IN THE VISUAL ARTS 79
    Artists who Loved Cats 80

LA CÉRAMIQUE-CERAMICS 91

DES ARMOIRIES À LA PUBLICITÉ -FROM COATS OF ARMS TO ADVERTISING 93

TRÈS BIZARRE!-VERY STRANGE 96
    Louis Coulon and his cuddly beard 97
    Cats in the Night Sky 97

LE FUTUR -THE FUTURE FOR FRENCH CATS 98
    "Juste les Essentiels, Madame" -The Facts, Ma'am, Just the Facts 99
    A New French Sub-Species: The Cat-Fox 100

MOVING TO FRANCE WITH YOUR CAT 101

EN GUISE DE CONCLUSION... -BY MEANS OF CONCLUSION... 103

L'AUTEUR -ABOUT THE AUTHOR--SÉAMUS MULLARKEY... 105

Preface

I'm very grateful you bought this book. Thanks so much for your support! I hope you enjoy it and that it is a welcome addition to your bookshelf. The Cats of France is a book in which I explore and document the history, folklore, and cultural significance of our French feline friends for all to enjoy.

Again, thanks so much…

Happy reading!

Séamus Mullarkey, July 2025

Introduction

Some say that in France, cats possess a certain *je ne sais quoi* that mirrors the nation itself—a unique combination of elegance, independence, and subtle superiority that seems almost bred into their very whiskers. Like the French appreciation for a perfectly aged Camembert or the ritual of the early evening apéritif, the relationship between France and its felines is based on centuries of mutual understanding and refined coexistence.

From the sun-drenched windowsills of Provence farmhouses to the wrought-iron balconies of Haussmann apartments in Paris, French cats have mastered the quintessentially Gallic art of living well. They embody that French disdain for hurried meals, preferring to savor their pâté (even if it comes from a can) with the same deliberate pleasure their human companions reserve for a leisurely two-hour lunch. Don't believe me? Simply watch a Parisian cat navigate the morning ritual at the local boulangerie—weaving between legs with aristocratic grace, accepting admiration as its natural due, yet maintaining just enough aloofness to preserve its mystique.

French cats are not mere pets but cultural ambassadors of French savoir-vivre—they know how to live well. These are creatures that understand intuitively that life should be lived with style, that comfort is a philosophy rather than mere luxury, and that a well-timed stretch in a patch of sunlight is worth more than all the frantic productivity of the Anglo-Saxon world. I would contend that they are the inheritors of a tradition that spans from medieval monastery mousers to the pampered companions of literary salons.

One of the most enchanting aspects of French culture is its deep connection to art, fashion, and literature—all fields where cats have left an indelible mark. From the whimsical illustrations of Théophile Steinlen to the sophisticated presence of cats in the haute couture of Coco Chanel, this book will explore how these elegant creatures have inspired and been immortalized by French creative geniuses. Moreover, we examine the lives of notable French cat lovers, including Colette and Victor Hugo, who found in their feline friends a source of comfort and inspiration.

In addition to their cultural impact, cats have also played practical roles in French society. They have worked as mousers in vineyards and kitchens, served as mascots in military units, and even acted as messengers during wartime. This book also celebrates the hardworking and often overlooked contributions of these industrious French cats.

La Luxe
- Fashion & Luxury

The King Who Built French Fashion

France has long been synonymous with effortless chic; a reputation rooted in the 17th century during the reign of Louis XIV. Known as the "Sun King," Louis XIV, along with his finance minister Jean-Baptiste Colbert, transformed France into the epicenter of luxury goods and fashion by establishing royal manufactories for textiles, tapestries, and glass, and by implementing strict regulations to ensure the highest quality craftsmanship. At the lavish court of Versailles, Louis XIV required his nobles to don sumptuous, meticulously crafted garments that had to be up to date, using fashion as a tool to assert political control, foster loyalty, and project French prestige across Europe. This had the effect of weakening the aristocrats who had to mortgage their estates to pay for ever-more extravagant outfits. This precarious financial position made them easier for the king to control. The rise of the fashion press in the late 17th century, with their descriptions and illustrations of the latest modes helped spread French styles far and wide, cementing Paris as the fashion capital of Europe. Notably, this period also saw the creation of the Parisian seamstresses' guild, granting women a significant role in the burgeoning luxury industry.

Choupette Le Chat

In 1910, Gabrielle Bonheur Chanel founded the modern French fashion house of Chanel. After Chanel's death in 1971, fashion designer Karl Lagerfeld became the creative director of the company and solidified the iconic interlocking "CC" image in fashion. Lagerfeld was well-known as not only a fashion designer, but also a massive cat lover. He had a blue cream Birman named Choupette, a common nickname for girls in France which means "cutie." Choupette was just a one-year-old kitty when she was gifted to the designer by French model Baptiste Giabiconi. Lagerfeld was only originally supported to cat-sit for the model, but it did not take long for him and the kitty he was looking after to become inseparable. Choupette the cat brought the designer great joy, and her official adoption was publicly announced in 2012 in V magazine.

The Cats of France

Referred to as "the most famous feline in the world," Choupette was featured in many fashion campaigns and even inspired her own haute couture collection for Chanel called "Choupette in Love." She received croquettes and pâté with every meal (served in separate dishes), and her two maids never failed to brush her twice a day, detailing the cat's daily activities in her personal diary which the designer could later review.

Choupette was named one of Karl Lagerfeld's heirs to his estate, and when he passed away in 2019, it was rumored that the designer left his fortune to his precious fur baby. The kitty was also given many designer gifts as condolences, and Lagerfeld's will stipulated that "la belle Choupette" was to be cared for by his long-trusted housekeeper, Françoise Caçote. Since Lagerfeld's death, Choupette's glamorous lifestyle has continued uninterrupted. She resides in a Parisian apartment with Caçote, her family, and another rescue cat named Siana. Choupette's routines remain as lavish as ever: she dines from fine Japanese porcelain bowls and even has her own miniature Louis Vuitton travel bag. She celebrated her 13th birthday at the Palace of Versailles, receiving an array of gifts including plush cushions, toys, and more porcelain bowls, all befitting her royal status.

Choupette's modeling career has flourished, with collaborations alongside supermodels like Naomi Campbell, Gisele Bündchen, and Kendall Jenner, and brand partnerships with the likes of Shu Uemura. The kitty's Instagram following exceeds 260,000, and she continues to captivate the fashion world, so much so that celebrities paid tribute to her at the 2023 Met Gala by dressing as cats

Having a princess-like temperament, Choupette decides when she wants to be brushed or photographed. Choupette is still treated like royalty, often napping on piles of Chanel clothing and traveling in style, just as she did with Lagerfeld on trips to glamorous French Riviera destinations like St. Tropez

Purr-fectly Chic: Louis Vuitton's Catogram Collection

In late 2018, Louis Vuitton celebrated the whimsical side of French luxury with its Catogram collection, a playful homage to feline charm that quickly became a sensation among both fashion lovers and cat enthusiasts. The collection was the result of a creative collaboration between Louis Vuitton's artistic director Nicolas Ghesquière and legendary fashion editor Grace Coddington, herself a devoted cat lover. Coddington's own Persian cats, Pumpkin and Blanket, were immortalized in her signature sketch style and emblazoned across iconic Louis Vuitton pieces, including bags, trunks, silk pajamas, and even shoes. The illustrations, featuring cats leaping and lounging atop the LV monogram, brought a sense of eccentric playfulness and warmth to the storied brand's heritage. For cat lovers, the Catogram line offered everything from cartoon-emblazoned coin purses to luxury luggage, proving that in France, even the world of haute couture has room for a bit of feline mischief.

Cats in French History

Cattus Romanus - The Latin legacy

The Ancient Romans first conquered France during the Gallic Wars in 52 BC under the command of Julius Caesar, inhabiting the country for 500 years from the 1st century BC until the 5th century AD. The Romans left their mark on France in many ways. They founded cities like Lyon, built roads and aqueducts that are still used today, and profoundly influenced the French language. Many words in modern French come from Latin. The French word for cat, "chat," is derived from the Latin word "cattus," which referred specifically to the domestic cat. Interestingly, an earlier Latin word, "feles," was used for wild cats and is the root of modern scientific and descriptive terms in French like "félin" (feline) and "félidé" (the cat family).

Latin also gave rise to a variety of related words: "catulus" and "catula" were diminutives that could mean "kitten" or "little cat," while "catella" also referred to a small animal or pet. The influence extends to modern French with words like "chaton" for kitten. Even affectionate nicknames for cats, such as "minou" and "minette," echo the tradition of diminutives found in Latin. Thus, the Latin language's legacy lives on not only in the everyday word for cat, but also in the rich array of feline-related terms to be found throughout the French language.

Cats at the Royal French Court

While dogs, horses, and exotic animals were the most prominent pets at the Palace of Versailles for much of its history, cats began to gain favor in the French royal court during the 17th and 18th centuries

The Cats of France

Pampered parliamentary pussycats were all the rage in the 1620s, largely due to one of the greatest French cat lovers of all time, Armand Jean du Plessis, Cardinal Richelieu. The cardinal was a French statesman and clergyman who became Foreign Secretary in 1616 and then served as the chief minister of France in 1624 until his death in 1642. He was a cat lover since childhood. His kitties would routinely romp around his office and sit on important documents such as maps. Richelieu kept two servants specifically to care for his precious kitty cats. Upon his death in 1642, Richelieu's will provided his fourteen precious remaining cats with caretakers who were bequeathed monetary allowances to care for the cats for the rest of their lives. Richelieu popularized cats as companion animals in fashionable French society. It was reported that around this time that many grand French chateaux started being built w chatières in their doors or what we would call cat flaps. Persians and Angoras were Richelieu's breeds of choice, and he is said to always have a cat in his lap. Amongst his many cats were Ludovic le Cruel, named for his dedication to killing rats; Ludoviska, who according to some sources was Ludovic's girlfriend and was Polish; Perruque (French for wig), named because she fell out of poet Honorat de Bueil's wig onto Richelieu's feet as a kitten, along with Pyrame and Thisbe, named after the lovers in Ovid's Metamorphoses because they slept while holding paws. *L'amour, toujours l'amour...*

Sketch based on Un Chat Angola *by French painter Jean-Jacques Bachelier*

It was under King Louis XIV that cats, especially the elegant long-haired Angora breed, became fashionable. Louis ascended to the throne at the age of five in 1643 and France was ruled on his behalf by the Duke of Orléans. However, the young king did attend to the Royal Council where state business was decided even though he didn't play an active part. During one of these drawn-out meetings, a kitten scampered across the table to the young king's delight and to the dismay of the courtiers. From then on, cats were often in attendance to keep the young king amused. Courtiers were a bit miffed at this feline participation as they felt it lowered the tone of serious political procedures.

The interest in cats wasn't only confined to royal circles but gained a hold across the French ruling classes. One case in point was the aristocrat Antoinette Du Ligier de la Garde Deshoulières (1638–1694). She was a French poet who was much admired by the most important literary figures of her time. Among her prodigious literary output were poems in the form of letters to the Duke of Vivonne's dog, Cochon, on behalf of her own cat, Grisette. She used this loving literary relationship between the two natural enemies to write a play, eventually published by her daughter as the tragedy-comedy *La mort de Cochon*, in which the cat Grisette's grief at her canine friend Cochon's death is mourned by a chorus of neighborhood tomcats.

The Cats of France

Louis XV (1710-1774) and his queen, Marie Leszczynska, were especially fond of Angoras, with white Angora cats becoming a court favorite. The king's majestic black cat, Général, was immortalized in a 1728 oil portrait by Jean-Baptiste Oudry, remarkable as the first known royal court painting to feature a cat as the main subject. Another celebrated royal feline, Brillant, was a large white Angora, referred to as "the King's colleague" and was given his own red cushion on the fireplace in the Council Cabinet to observe royal meetings. Indeed, cats could do no wrong at the court, and Queen Marie Lesczynska's dismissive response when a court lady complained that the queen's cat had destroyed a fur-lined cloak was that the complaining aristocrat should have placed her precious garment out of the cat's reach.

Marie Antoinette, the last queen of France before the Revolution, was also known to keep Angora cats. According to a popular (but preposterous) legend, while her plans to escape France during the Revolution failed, several of her cherished long-haired cats were sent ahead on a ship bound for America, along with some of her belongings. The story goes that these cats landed in Maine, where they are said to have interbred with local cats and became the ancestors of the Maine Coon, the large, long-haired breed now famous in the United States. While the legend of Marie Antoinette's cats adds a romantic twist to the story of the Maine Coon, it remains just that, an improbable legend.

La cuisine - Michelin Star Kitties in the Kitchen

The Cats of France

French haute cuisine, or "high cuisine," has roots stretching back to the lavish medieval banquets of French royalty and nobility, with their focus on elaborate presentations and the finest ingredients. Over the centuries, French cooking absorbed influences from Roman techniques, Renaissance Italy, and global trade, gradually evolving into a refined culinary tradition marked by complex sauces and precise methods. Key figures like François Pierre La Varenne in the 17th century and Auguste Escoffier in the 19th century codified and elevated these techniques, making French cuisine the global benchmark for fine dining. While haute cuisine was historically reserved for the elite, France's passion for food appreciation extends to all levels of society— even ordinary French schools cultivate children's palates with multi-course lunches, nutrition education, and lessons on food culture and sustainability. This national reverence for food, from the grandest restaurants to the school canteen, is central to French identity.

A star from Le Guide Michelin, or The Michelin Guide, is the most prestigious honor a restaurant can receive as recognition of its culinary excellence. With a rating system of one, two, or three stars (three being the highest), each Michelin Star represents how worthy a restaurant is of a special trip just to sample its culinary delights. This rating system originated in 1900 when the French tire company Michelin created the guidebook to promote travel across France in the then new-fangled automobiles. The culinary award is now recognized internationally.

On August 22, 1993, The New York Times magazine recognized two exceptional restaurants out of nineteen that were awarded the coveted rating of three stars by Le Guide Michelin. Both restaurants, Troisgros and L'Esperance, are in Burgundy, just two hours east of Paris, a region that's known for its delectable wines. These two restaurants are also known for their feline inhabitants, Mitou and Tricotine.

In the New York Times article France's 3-Star Cats: A Vanishing Breed, Mr. Troisgros, head chef and head of the family who owned the three-star restaurant Troisgros, remarked that they "have always had cats." His grandfather had a white cat named Dodo who always stretched out across his shoulders. At that time, Troisgrois was just a small cafe, and not yet a Michelin hotel-restaurant complex. The Troisgrois family always made sure to feed any stray cats that came to their business. The restaurant even had twenty-three cats that ate there regularly at one point! At the time of the article Troisgros, now a hotel as well as a restaurant, had one cat: Tricotine.

Tricotine, a distinguished calico, was adopted by Troisgros when she showed up one day at their doorstep pregnant with a broken tail. She ended up being taken care of by restaurant director Gerard Joubert, who found homes for her kittens and arranged for her spaying and tail tip amputation. Tricotine continued to live like a stray cat at times, darting along the busy street, but always returning home in time for dinner at Troisgrois. There, she always had a seat at the family's table. Joubert supervised her strolls in front of the city hotel and fed her twice a day under the serving table in her favorite part of the dining room. Tricotine also got a chicken breast when there was an extra one, but she wouldn't eat salmon.

Three hours from Troisgros is another three-star Michelin French restaurant that was home to a special kitchen cat, Mitou. This poised grey cat with a round head and white stripes over her front legs, was the kitty resident of restaurant L'Esperance near Vezelay in north central France. Also, a stray of humble beginnings, then Mitou began visiting this three-star restaurant-hotel. She quickly adapted to her new grand home. In the evenings before dinnertime, Mitou could be found sitting at the top of the steps leading into the restaurant or snuggling into her favourite gray chair at the receptionist's desk.

The chef's mother, Mrs. Meneau fed the pampered kitty "the best and freshest meat and fish, just as they come in" such as minced lotte, the same fish they use to create the restaurant's famous dish Lotte au Quinquin. Apparently, in France, it is necessary to not only eat well yourself but ensure that your local kittens also enjoy scrumptious treats! The chef, Marc Meneau, was quoted as saying, "my mother gives this cat too much to eat, food that's too rich—against my orders." However, the chef said that it's an important aspect of French culture to have a cat around the restaurant. It is thanks to Mitou that Meneau's family restaurant remained free from rodents for years. And so, in return, it is the duty of Meneau to create delicious meals, not just for its patrons but also for its four-pawed guests. These kitchen kitties are a dying breed, since sanitation regulations forbid all animals from professional kitchens for health reasons, so nowadays they just wander around the rest of the premises.

La guerre - Military Kitties

Sketch of regimental cat near Cambrin, France, 1918

World War I

Cats are our loyal and trustworthy companions during the best of times and the worst of times. This includes the unfortunate events of war whose horrors no cat or human should ever encounter. Trench warfare in World War I (1914-1918) was primarily in an area in northern France and Belgium, known as the Western Front. It saw combat between German troops and the Allied forces of France, Great Britain, and eventually the United States. The two sides faced each other with an area in between that would be subjected to firepower from both sides. This area was labelled "no man's land." Each army dug a series of trenches in which to shelter from the gunfire of the other side. Over time the trenches became damp and dirty, a perfect breeding ground for rats and disease. Luckily there were brave feline mousers who also provided a large boost in morale, the trench cats! There were an estimated 500,000 such cats employed throughout the Western Front's trench systems in WWI.

Aside from pest control, these kitties boosted morale by becoming mascots for troops who would be fed and played with by the soldiers. Heroically but heart-wrenchingly, the trench cats were also early detectors of the near colorless, toxic and odorless chemical gases used during the war. Like canaries in a mineshaft, the illness and deaths of these cats would alert nearby troops to the presence of the gas, a warning which would save countless GI lives.

Another job for the heroic kitties was as messengers. A cat named Choux travelled the war zones from France to Germany to deliver a message from his owner announcing the birth of a child.

During the famous Christmas Truce of 1914, a cat, known as Felix to the Allies and Nestor to the Germans, became an informal messenger, carrying friendly notes across no man's land between opposing trenches. This feline go-between was cherished by soldiers on both sides for his role in fostering brief moments of camaraderie. However, after military authorities discovered Felix's activities, he was arrested and executed for treason, a tragic fate reflecting the paranoia and harsh discipline of wartime. Felix's story, a testament to the absurdity of war, inspired by an anti-war poem by Heathcote Williams and is alluded to in the 2005 film Joyeux Noel, where a cat is accused of espionage (but spared the execution on screen that did occur in real life). Often, the good deeds of such brave cats go unnoticed, but Felix remains a symbol of peace and the small acts of humanity to be found even amid conflict.

Heathcote Williams: The Cat Who Was Shot for Treason

A cat was shot for treason

In World War One.

It had acted as an intermediary

Between Allied and Axis lines:

Soldiers could send messages

To each other

By tying scraps of paper

To the cat's collar.

The cat then ran across No Man's Land,

From one trench to the other.

World War II

During World War II, cats played a crucial role in France as guardians of food stores, tasked with keeping vital supplies safe from rodents. Their talent for hunting vermin was so valued that many military and civilian cats received extra rations, such as powdered milk, in recognition of their service. The devastation of the war, including bombings and mass displacement, led to a sharp decline in the domestic animal population throughout France. Many pets were lost, abandoned, or perished in chaos.

This shortage of cats became a real problem, as unchecked rodent populations threatened already scarce food supplies. To combat this, the United States launched the "Cats for Europe" campaign, sending thousands of American cats across the Atlantic to help control vermin in French towns, cities, and countryside. These American alley cats, prized for their hardiness and skill, were enlisted to fill the gap left by the decimated local cat population and quickly became unsung heroes of the home front. It's interesting to note that many of the current-day French cat population may have American ancestry!

Paysages et Monuments - Landscapes and Landmarks

Catwalks of the Middle Ages: Strolling Down Ruelle des Chats

If you find yourself journeying through the Champagne region of France, don't miss the enchanting Ruelle des Chats in the city of Troyes—a highlight for both cat lovers and history buffs. Troyes, the historic capital of Aube and officially designated a City of Art and History, is renowned for its beautifully preserved medieval architecture. The Ruelle des Chats, or "Alley of the Cats," is a narrow, cobbled passageway whose origins date back to the 15th century. After the devastating Great Fire of 1524, much of Troyes was rebuilt, and the alley's distinctive half-timbered houses were restored so that the upper floors nearly touch. The alley earned its whimsical name of Alley of the Cats because the rooftops are so close that, as local legend has it, cats could leap from one rooftop to another without ever touching the ground. As you stroll through the half-light of this charming lane, you might spot playful cat statues or even a carved cat's face among the beams—details that pay tribute to the alley's feline namesakes and add to its magical atmosphere.

Graveyard Gardens & Graffiti

Cemeteries aren't the first destination to come to mind as additions to your tourist itinerary. Yet, according to author of Les chats de Paris, Barnaby Conrad the Third, Père-Lachaise Cemetery is the "best place to see cats" in Paris. Wandering around the famous resting places of Chopin, Oscar Wilde, Proust, Marcel Marceau and Jim Morrison are a population of about fifty or so feral felines that call this necropolis their home. Père-Lachaise Cemetery, established in 1804, is Paris's largest cemetery at 44 hectares (or 110 acres) and was the city's first landscaped burial ground. It is regarded today as having a "rich ecosystem" and has become a miniature biodiversity reserve.

Located nearly 30 minutes away by Metro from Père-Lachaise Cemetery in Montmartre Cemetery is Paris's third largest cemetery and also home to a clan of cats. Among the tombs of the likes of famous French notables, such as painter Edgar Degas and actress Jeanne Moreau, is a thriving cat population of around fifty stray but friendly cats that can be seen stretching out to sunbathe on and amongst the graves and tombstones. Famous cat lover and French author, Théophile Gautier, also rests in Montmartre Cemetery where a carved cat forms part of his headstone.

Feline Street Art

If these cemetery cats are too elusive for you to photograph, there is kitty street art that will sit still for some good pics. M. Chat, also known as Monsieur or Mr. Chat is an orange-yellow, grinning, cartoon-esque cat graphic that originated in Orléans with artist Thoma Vuille. It can be seen painted on more than eighty walls in Paris, including a concentration along the Porte de Clignancourt / Porte d'Orléans axis. Another street artist, Alberto Vejarano or Chanoir (an abbreviation for chat noir) creates works of cartoon cats wearing hats. Some of these can be seen in Paris, notably one near Saint Ambroise church on rue de la Folie Méricourt. Another famous example of cats in Paris street art is the black and blue stencil mural of a cat looking to the side by artist Christian Guémy, aka C215, which can be found on the side of a building near the Paris Nationale Metro.

Sketch of M. Chat graffiti

Les Races Félines - Cat Breeds

Chartreux male cat presented at the Vantaa cat show 2008

Chartreux: The uniquely French breed

This breed of cat with blue-gray fur and large, golden or copper eyes seems to have originated in the southeast of France near the city of Grenoble. They are known for their tapered muzzles that give this breed an appearance of "smiling," and a thick wooly coat with even coloring. Some rumors say that the kitties were gifted to Carthusian monks at La Grande Chartreuse monastery by knights returning from the Middle East (modern-day Syria and Cyprus) during the Crusades. First referred to as "The Chartreux Cats" by the 1723 Bruslon's Universal Dictionary, the breed was also referred to as the "blue cat of France," "monastery Cats," and "smiling cats."

Starting in 1928, the Leger Sisters executed highly selective breeding of the Chartreux cats on the island of Belle Ile en Mer, and the breed was officially exhibited in Paris in 1931. Although the breeding program experienced setbacks during World War II, a massive comeback in the 1970s spread the popularity of The Chartreux across the seas to the United States.

A lean and muscular cat with bony limbs, this blue cat is incredibly playful, intelligent, and friendly. They get along well with children and other animals, but they must be well-trained to not push boundaries with their active behavior. The Chartreux tend to prefer being in charge, however they are also a quiet creature who enjoys their solitude and independence. Perhaps the most notable enthusiast of the breed was General Charles de Gaulle, the President of France during the mid-20th century. He referred to his beloved kitty as "Gris-Gris" (gray-gray).

- One of the oldest natural cat breeds and originating from France, the Chartreux is the National Cat of France.

- Some cat fanciers lovingly refer to the Chartreux as a "potato on toothpicks" due to their fine-boned legs with stocky bodies and round, "grinning" faces.

- Joachim du Bellay was the first to mention the Chartreux in a 1558 poem entitled *Vers Français sur la mort d'un petit chat*, or "French verse on the death of a small cat."

Serrade Petit

The Serrade Petit is a recently discovered breed that has yet to be standardized by any cat breed associations. While it is unknown exactly how this breed appeared, their presence is highly prominent in France to the point that any person looking to obtain one will have a difficult time finding any outside of the country. As the name suggests, Serrade Petit cats are quite little with a delicate body structure and even tinier paws. They have small heads with disproportionally large, erect ears, round eyes, and soft, short hair that can be tan, gray, white, or orange.

Blessed with pleasant personalities, these cats have an ideal balance of mild and playful spirit. While they enjoy their fair share of fun-time, they tend to have a less frantic energy than other breeds. It's certainly not uncommon to find these little kitties bundled up on the laps of their loved ones. The Serrade Petit are not a shy breed and will not hesitate to voice their humble opinions if their needs are not met. Plenty of mews and cries will ensue if they are ignored or left alone for too long.

These cats are quite intelligent and require a variety of enrichment to prevent boredom. Serrade Petit cats are best suited as indoor pets and are rare outside France. They are generally good with families and children and may get along with other pets if socialized early.

Birman - mythical origins in Burma but modern origins in France

Despite their mystical legends of temple origins in Burma (nowadays Myanmar), the Birman cat as we know it today is deeply entwined with French history. The breed's modern story begins on the French Riviera in the early 1920s, when a female named Poupee de Madalpour, believed to be pregnant on arrival, became the foundation of the breed in Europe. France officially recognized the "Sacré de Birmanie" as a distinct breed in 1925, and it was French breeders who carefully shaped the Birman's signature look: striking sapphire-blue eyes, creamy coats with darker points, and their iconic white "gloves" on each paw

The Birman's survival is a testament to French dedication. The breed was nearly wiped out during World War II, with only two known survivors, Orloff and Xenia de Kaabaa, remaining in France. Through careful outcrossing and selective breeding, French enthusiasts rebuilt the population, ensuring the Birman's gentle temperament and elegant appearance lived on. Today, while the breed's name pays homage to its legendary Burmese roots, the Birman's true renaissance and international acclaim are thanks to the passion and perseverance of French breeders, making it as much a part of France's feline heritage as the Chartreux.

Institutions Françaises - French Institutions

Les Chats du Ministère: When French Bureaucracy Meets Feline Flair

When faced with a stubborn rat problem in their ministry buildings, French officials did something delightfully French—they brought in two cats, Nomi and Noé, to prowl the halls as official mousers. Instead of calling in exterminators or relying solely on traps, they opted for a solution that's both practical and charming. It's the kind of move you'd expect from a country that treasures its heritage and isn't afraid to add a touch of whimsy to even the most bureaucratic settings. In a way, the sight of sleek cats padding through the corridors of power says a lot about French civil service: it's serious about getting things done, but always with a nod to culture and understated wit.

Hospitals and Nursing Homes

Regularly ranked among the world's best, France's healthcare system is renowned for its holistic approach, blending conventional Western medicine with therapies like rest cures and thalassotherapy, seaside treatments using mineral-rich seawater. In a country where relaxation and prevention are part of the prescription, it's no wonder the French have also welcomed therapy cats into hospitals and care homes, embracing the healing power of animal companionship as part of patient well-being. Projet Thérapattes (Project Therapy-Paws) is a French program founded by Chats du Quercy. This modern-day therapeutic program offers abandoned cats a second chance for love (*toujours l'amour!*). Thérapattes place cats in retirement or day centers to stimulate and comfort sufferers of Alzheimer's disease, depression, or those with disabilities. From children to seniors, these kitties offer companionship and a way to increase the quality and quantity of patients' social interactions.

Les Grands Amants des Chats - Major French Cat Lovers

Joachim Du Bellay and his lament for his cat

Du Bellay was one of the founders of La Pléiade, a group of 16th century French Renaissance poets who wished to elevate the status of French language to that of the classical tongues of Latin and Greek. Their end goal was to validate French as a language for poetry and literature. Du Bellay and his peers were met with pushback from attackers who called the translations of Latin poems to French as mere imitations and a show of ingratitude toward their predecessors. Du Bellay may have sought comfort from this public criticism with his feline friend. His beloved cat companion was called Gris Argentin Petit Belaud (what a name!) or "silver-grey little Belaud." This kitty shared the poet's bed and ate at his table like a proper gentleman. Of course, this beloved feline made its way into Du Bellay's poems too. Below is an excerpt of Du Bellay's memorial poem for the precious pussy cat.

Excerpt from Epitaph on a Cat

Oh, Good Lord, what pleasant fun

'Twas to watch my Belaud run

Swiftly for a ball of thread,

Or when chose his merry head

After his own tail to race

Round and round in wheeling chase

Michel de Montaigne

"Man's superiority over the animals is a delusion based on pride."
— Michel de Montaigne

Born in 1533 at Château de Montaigne, aristocrat and statesman Michel Eyquem, Seigneur de Montaigne or more commonly known as Michel de Montaigne, is regarded as one of the most influential writers of the French Renaissance. He is thought to have popularized the essay or *essai* as a literary genre. The word essay originated from the French word *essai* which means "to try" or "attempt" and means writings that try to explore thoughts or ideas. Montaigne wrote explorations into his own psyche about everyday things or events such as the correct way to exit a dinner party, horseback riding, marriage, kidney stones…and cats.

In his essay *An Apology for Raymond Sebond*, there is a highly regarded passage about his pet cat in which Montaigne writes about humanity's vanity to feel superior to animals. He wonders whether playtime with his cat is more of a case of his cat playing with him, than him playing with the cat… What a head-scratcher! What do you think? Writing from another creature's viewpoint (and recognizing sentience in animals) and casting doubt on the knowledge and power of man gave the world a new perspective that shattered preconceptions about animals. Merci, Montaigne!

Madame Dupuis

Harpist Madame Dupuis, a well-known musician of her day, bequeathed most of her fortune to her cats upon her death in 1677. Her will contained very specific instructions outlining their care and feeding. She allocated her sister, Marie Bluteau, and her niece, Madame Calonge, thirty sous a week (about fifty US dollars in 2025) so they could look after the kitties. Every day, they were to be served two meals of meat soup with bread broken into squares the size of a nut (otherwise the cats apparently would refuse to eat it) and finely minced meat. The dish was to be mildly seasoned and simmered in a covered, clean pan before being served in an individual soup plate for each of the pampered felines. The will ends with the final clause: "Nicole-Pigeon is to take charge of my two cats, and to be very careful of them. Madame Calonge is to visit them three times a week." However, angry relatives protested and won the case against Madame Dupius's now money-less mousers. The case was so eccentric that it was considered a cause célèbre and was mentioned by various contemporary writers such as Moncrief and Mercier St. Leger.

Moncrif's Les Chats

"Green eyes inspire grand passions only, and nature, which has refused them to the beauties of this century, has lavished them on the cat species." — Francois-Augustin Paradis de Moncrif

François-Augustin de Paradis de Moncrif was a French writer, musician, actor, and poet born in Paris in 1687 to a family of French and Scottish origins. He was also appointed as King Louis XV's historiographer royal or the historian of the court. Although he wasn't such a well-known writer at the time, he gained recognition with his now famous book, Les Chats published in 1727. The volume consisted of letters and poems devoted to cats and was the first major study of cats.

In Les Chats Moncrif staunchly defends the noble creatures. He wrote that although many believe that "Cats are treacherous by nature, that they suffocate infants" and "are sorcerers," those with reason can find that "there is none among the animals who can bear more brilliant titles than those of the cat species." Unfortunately, Moncrif was completely ahead of his time, as the publication was met with ridicule and mockery. Years later Moncrif was admitted to the Academie Française, a highly prestigious body which serves as France's official authority on the French language. This institution is in charge of laying down standards for grammar, vocabulary and language usage and is a source of great national pride in France. Some of Moncrif's fellow members looked down on him as a non-serious writer because he wrote about, of all things, plain old kitty cats. At Moncrif's admission ceremony to the academy, a colleague smuggled a poor cat into the induction ceremony and let it loose as Moncrif was giving his admission speech. The moment the scared feline let out a pitiful meow, the audience of pretentious academicians began to also meow in mockery of Moncrif.

The cruelty of his peers forced Moncrif to later remove Les Chats from circulation and delete it from his collected works. Ironically, the book is now prized as the forerunner of feline literature while his other works and many of those of his peers are mostly forgotten. Moncrif's last words in the book rang especially true, "one day we shall see the merit of cats generally recognized. It is impossible that in a nation as enlightened as France that the prejudice in this regard should prevail much longer."

Alexandre Dumas

Born in 1802 and author of The Three Musketeers and The Count of Monte Cristo, Alexandre Dumas is known for his love for his cats, Mysouff I, Mysouff II, and Le Docteur. He boldly declared that (apologies to dog lovers!) "Rather than a dog, I would choose a cat. It has for me the manners essential to social relations."

The prolific French novelist claimed that Mysouff I was psychic and could tell when Dumas was coming home. The cat would walk Dumas to a specific spot on his way to work and would be there upon his return like clockwork. Somehow Mysouff I could tell when Dumas would be late and could be found sleeping during those days. Dumas' black and white cat, Mysouff II, was his favorite even though one fateful day the cat ate all the author's exotic birds. Dumas held a mock trial in the presence of some house guests and sentenced the cat to five years' imprisonment, during which time he would share a cage with the monkey that had given the cat access to the aviary. Luckily for Mysouff II, Dumas fell on hard times and had to sell all his monkeys.

Victor Hugo

"Everybody has noticed the way cats stop and loiter in a half-open door. Hasn't everyone said to a cat: For heaven's sake why don't you come in?" — Victor Hugo

Victor Hugo (1805-1885) was one of the most acclaimed authors in the history of French literature and author of Les Misérables. This French poet, novelist, and playwright lived in exile until the fall of Napoleon III and was greatly fond of cats. He wrote lovingly in his diary of his cats Mouche and Gavroche (later renamed Chanoine). Hugo is quoted as saying: "God has made the cat to give man the pleasure of caressing the tiger." and "the cat is a drawing-room tiger."

Gavroche or Chanoine was a "magnificent Angora" and Hugo's favorite. Gavroche loved sitting on a dais or throne of crimson satin. On Hugo's granddaughter's birthday, he presented her with the lovely angora Gavroche who held in his paws a large bouquet of flowers with a note that said, "From Gavroche, Boulevard de la Mére-Michel." Obviously, it must have been written by ravroche himself.

Théophile Gautier

The dog may be wonderful prose, but only the cat is poetry — Gautier

Théophile Gautier adored cats and wrote a book about his domestic life with cats titled *Ménagerie Intime*. Born in 1811, this famous French poet, novelist, and critic owned many a feline furrball. Gautier did not neuter any of his cats and so the number in his home grew greater and greater. Gautier's first cat, Childebrand, was a black and tan tabby. Madame Théophile was a reddish cat with blue eyes and a white breast who hated listening to high notes (especially the high A). She would follow Gautier on his walks, snatch a morsel or two right off his fork at the dinner table, and sleep in Gautier's bed. Eponine was a black cat named after a character in Hugo's *Les Miserables* who loved listening to female singers. When he dined alone, Gautier would have a place set at the table for Eponine. When he arrived at the table, she would already be there with her paws neatly folded on the tablecloth "like a well-bred little girl [...]." He wrote, "She went right through the dinner, dish by dish, from soup to dessert, waiting for her turn to be helped, and behaving with such propriety and nice manners as one would like to see in many children." Eponine wasn't the only one of Gautier's cats with a distinctive personality. He had a kitten named Cléopatre who liked standing on three legs. Zizi was the musician of the family, who composed her best work while walking across the piano at night.

Above Gautier's resting place in Paris's Montmartre Cemetery is a carved cat on his headstone watching all who pass by. In one of Gautier's writings, he describes the cat as "a philosophical, methodical, quiet animal, tenacious of his own habits, fond of order and cleanliness, and does not lightly confer his friendship. If you are worthy of his affection, a cat will be your friend but never your slave." *Comme c'est vrai!* How true that is!

Charles Baudelaire

Charles Baudelaire was born in 1821 Paris, France to middle-class parents. Although his stepfather wanted to place Baudelaire in a career of law or diplomacy, Baudelaire decided to pursue a literary path. The young Charles frequented prostitutes and ran up debts. His most famous work, *Les Fleurs du Mal*, deals with themes such beauty, eroticism, boredom, and the modern city...

At 21, Baudelaire received an inheritance that he quickly squandered. The writer often moved to avoid endlessly chasing creditors. Throughout his unsettled life, Baudelaire found joy and comfort in the company of cats. Below is one of his poems from *Les Fleurs du Mal*. Can any of you relate to Baudelaire's *amour fou* for his feline companions?

Le Chat by Charles Baudelaire	The Cat - Translated by William Aggeler
Viens, mon beau chat, sur mon coeur amoureux;	Come, my beautiful cat, to my amorous heart;
Retiens les griffes de ta patte,	Hold back the claws of your paw,
Et laisse-moi plonger dans tes beaux yeux,	And let me gaze into your beautiful eyes
Mêlés de métal et d'agate.	Of metal and agate.
Lorsque mes doigts caressent à loisir	When my fingers leisurely caress you,
Ta tête et ton dos élastique,	Your head and your elastic back,
Et que ma main s'enivre du plaisir	And when my hand tingles with the pleasure
De palper ton corps électrique.	Of feeling your electric body.

The Cats of France

Pierre Loti

French novelist and naval officer Pierre Loti was born in Rochefort in 1850, a city in Southwestern France. Loti was known for his eccentricity, even preposterously claiming to the Académie Française, the guardians of French language and literature, in 1892 that "Loti ne sait pas lire" or "Loti doesn't know how to read;" Loti had already written several novels in the decade or so prior!

Most of Loti's works related to his travels in the French Navy, but one of his works was focused on his life with his two cats. Lives of Two Cats first appeared in English in 1900 and was written about Loti's felines, Moumoutte Blanche and Moumoutte Chinoise. Blanche was Loti's black and white Angora that had already been with him for some years before Chinois came around. Chinois was a stowaway kitten Loti brought home after a trip to China and as we all know, introducing an unfamiliar feline to another can get a bit…finicky. Apparently the two cats immediately attacked each other so savagely upon introduction that Loti had to pour water on the fierce felines to separate them. Luckily, they hated being soaked so much that they never fought again. *Quelle bonne idée*! What a good solution!

sketch based on Rousseau's portrait *Loti with His Cat*

Sketch of Colette and her cats

Colette

One of the truly famous group of individuals, immediately identifiable by her first name, Colette, the French author is quoted as saying, "Making friends with a cat can only be a profitable experience." Born in 1873 in the village of Saint-Sauveur-en-Puisaye in the department of Yonne, Burgundy, Colette was also a mime, actress, and journalist. She devoted herself to her furry friends and wrote about her cats in her many books. Her cat, Kiki-la-Doucette featured as a talking cat debating life with a French bulldog in her 1903 work Sept Dialogues de Bêtes (Seven Dialogues with Animals).

Colette felt strongly about the positives of owning a cat, writing "The only risk you ever run in befriending a cat is enriching yourself," and that "there are no ordinary cats." She wrote many stories in which the main characters were cats such as in her 1933 novel, simply titled, Le Chat. The book focuses on the complex relationships between a man, woman, and a cat. The story ends with the man, Alain, leaving his jealous wife, Camille, when she tries fatally injuring his cat that he's loved since his childhood. In the non-literary sphere, Colette collaborated with French composer Maurice Ravel to produce the opera L'Enfant et les Sortiléges." This romantic duet between two cats had its first performance in 1925.

Jean Cocteau

Jean Cocteau (1889–1963), known as the "Prince Frivole," was a leading figure in early 20th-century Surrealist, Dada, and avant-garde circles. In 1947, he and actor Jean Marais acquired a historic 16th-century stone house with an adjoining medieval chapel in Milly la Forêt, south of Paris. Cocteau adorned the Saint Blaise des Simples Chapel with whimsical murals—plants, Christ, saints—and even a cat symbolizing resurrection above Cocteau's tomb. An avid cat lover, he was regularly photographed with his beloved felines, including Karoun and Madeleine, and famously said, "I love cats… they become the visible soul of a home."

Charles de Gaulle

Charles André Joseph Marie de Gaulle was born in 1890 in Lille, a city in northern France. He is commonly known as le Général de Gaulle or simply as le Général (the General). Le Général led the Free French Forces against Nazi Germany during WWII and was key to restoring democracy in France after the dissolution of the Third Republic. De Gaulle absolutely adored his precious gray chartreux named Gris-Gris. The Chartreux is one of the rarest breeds in the world, with most of its population decimated during both World Wars. De Gaulle's wife and First Lady of France, Yvonne de Gaulle bought a Chartreux during de Gaulle's second term as President. De Gaulle was captivated by the handsome cat and its strong personality. Who can blame him?

The cat originally had Ringo de Balmalon as its pedigree name but was renamed Gris-Gris by de Gaulle as a play on words, meaning gray-gray in French for its coloration but also referring to African lucky charms, which are called gris-gris. Gris-Gris followed the President from room to room and accompanied him devotedly on his walks. The precious gray kitty even made his way into conversations with the Minister of Cultural Affairs, André Malraux who was also a lover of cats and had two of his own, Lustrée and Fourrure (glossy and furry). In a lighthearted exchange with Malraux, de Gaulle mused "Kittens play, Cat meditate," undoubtedly inspired by Gris-Gris…

Les Ennemis des Chats
-Boo, Hiss! Those Cat Haters

It's not easy being beautiful, popular, and adored by millions. You see, along with cat lovers, also come a few haters. Honestly, even cat lovers can sometimes find their fluffy furballs annoying, whether it be from crossing personal boundaries or scratching up furniture. We know they aren't always perfect little gremlins.

According to 1700s French naturalist Georges Louis Leclerc de Buffon in his 1767 Natural History, cats apparently possess "an innate malice and perverse disposition which increase as they grow up, and which education teaches them to conceal but not to subdue. From determined robbers, the best education can only convert them into flattering thieves…they have only the appearance of attachment or friendship." Mmm, this writer certainly was a bit of cat hater and such dislike has a scientific term for it. Yes, ailurophobia is the deep-seated fear and/or hate of cats generally from childhood trauma. Some root causes could be from an unpleasant but shocking discovery of teeth or claws as a child or an irrational fear built-up by parents or family that the cat may harm the baby or child. Popular legend has it that the best-known French ailurophobe or scaredy-cat was Napoleon. Apparently, the military hero and ruler of France was retiring to bed one night when he was heard screaming for help. One of his aides came to his rescue only to find that there was un petit chaton, a tiny kitten, hiding behind the tapestry that hung on the wall. Napoleon was in a state of panic, sweating profusely and lunging wildly with fear with his sword at the tapestry until the harmless feline could be removed.

Les Chats dans les Traditions Populaires
- The Cat in French Folklore

Sketch of le chat botté, or Puss and Boots in English

The Black Cat Cure

There is a popular legend in France in which a knight travels to the town of Metz during a terrible epidemic of St. Vitus's Dance. As befits the name, the illness caused villagers to twitch and jump in grotesque dance-like movements. One evening, an enormous black cat appears before the knight. He immediately drew his sword which scared off the cat. The moment the cat ran off, everyone in the village was miraculously and magically cured. This idea coincides with the negative connotations black cats carried up until the late 1600s, implying the cat brought about misfortune and that scaring it away would remove bad luck.

The Matagot

In the southern provinces of France, black cats are believed to bring good luck if cared for properly, a belief rooted in the rich folklore of the magical creature known as the matagot. The matagot is a legendary, shape-shifting spirit that may appear as a rat, dog, fox, or cow, but its most famous and sought-after form is that of a black cat, often called the "money cat" or *chat d'argent* in regions like Gascony and Provence. According to tradition, the matagot can bestow fortune and prosperity upon its owner, but this beneficial relationship is conditional: the cat must be treated with the utmost respect, provided a comfortable box to sleep in, and, most importantly, always be given the first bite of every meal. Folklore warns that neglecting or mistreating a matagot can bring swift misfortune. Some tales even describe elaborate rituals to acquire a matagot, such as luring it at a crossroads with a plump chicken and carrying it home in silence, never looking back. In some versions, the matagot is seen as a domestic spirit that guards the home or barn, while in others, it is a more diabolical being, said to serve sorcerers or witches in exchange for their souls

The White Cat Princess

"The Prince and the White Cat" is a French fable that tells of a king who sends his three sons to find the perfect dog; the winner will inherit the throne. During their quest, the youngest prince, who is notably handsome and amiable, gets lost and finds himself at a lavish palace. Guided inside by mysterious forces, he meets a white cat who promises safety. The two dine and grow close, and the prince nearly forgets his mission.

Over time, the white cat (who was previously a princess until she was cursed and became feline) provides magical solutions to the youngest prince, in response to his father, the king's increasingly difficult challenges to his sons, including producing a cloth fine enough to pass through a needle's eye. When the king challenges his sons to bring back the most beautiful lady, the white cat instructs the prince to transform her back into a princess by cutting off her head and her tail. The fairies had turned her into a cat when her parents had reneged on a promise they had made. The prince is understandably reluctant, but she insists that doing so will turn her back into a princess. Her word comes true and after the prince has carried out the barbaric act, she does indeed turn into the loveliest of princesses and the prince presents her to his father. At this stage the king had planned to give his kingdom to the prince who had found the loveliest princess. The white cat princess, realizing that this will cause further strife reveals that she is the possessor of several kingdoms of her own and bestows a kingdom on each the prince's brothers, demonstrating that this formerly feline royal is generous and fair as well as beautiful beyond compare.

La Fontaine's Raminagrobis, Raton, and Rodilard

Born in 1621 at Château-Thierry in France, Jean de La Fontaine was a French fabulist or fable writer and one of the most widely read French poets of the 17th century. His well-known fables became a model for other writers across Europe. In his many works, de la Fontaine has recurring feline characters such as Raminagrobis, Raton, and Rodilard.

Raminagrobis was as large as his name. This fat, reclusive cat appears in several tales with a predatory greed that overshadows all else. For instance, when considering how to settle a dispute between two creatures, he opted to eat them both!

Raton, another one of Fontaine's fictional cats, is from a cautionary tale of a monkey and a cat. The monkey flatters Raton the kitty into pulling hot chestnuts out of a fire with its paw. As each nut is pawed out, the monkey quickly eats them. The animals are then disturbed and the monkey flees, ditching Raton to ponder the value of flattery and bemoan his burned paws.

Rodilard appears in two of Fontaine's 17th century fables as a cunning, predatory cat who is incredibly successful in his ventures. In the stories, the kitty is in the midst of battle with a colony of mice. In one of the tales, a council of rodents decides that Rodilard needs a bell tied around his neck to alert them when he approaches. However they have a problem, who is going to "bell the cat?" As cats are known as very successful hunters, I wouldn't volunteer if I were one of them. In the other tale, Rodilard plays dead to catch the mice and then uses flour to cunningly camouflage himself.

Charles Perrault's Puss in Boots

Born in 1628, French lawyer and author Charles Perrault gave the world retellings of various old stories such as Little Red Riding Hood, Cinderella, Sleeping Beauty, and, of course, Puss in Boots. Perrault created a number of tales to amuse his children. He became the leading member of the Académie Française and also laid the foundations for the new (at the time) literary genre, the fairy tale. His works were derived from old half-forgotten, traditional folktales with hazy origins that he retold in a simpler and more compelling form. These works were published in his 1697 book *Histoires ou contes du temps passé* (Stories or Tales from Past Times), later released in English in 1729. Perrault's version of Puss in Boots or Le Maître Chat ou le chat botté is considered the definitive one.

Puss in Boots, also known as The Master Cat, proved to be a major influence in changing the negative image of cats at the time because the cat was depicted as a clever animal rather than an evil creature. Up until then, because of the Middle Ages and the Christian Church, it was common to view the cat as related to witches and the devil.

The story begins with a dying miller who divides his property between his three sons but he leaves his youngest with only the granary cat who guards the grain stores. This poor young man's only possession is the cat so he decides that his only option is to eat the cat and wear its skin. Since that is definitely not in the cat's interests, the cat persuades the young man that wealth will come if the young man has boots made for the cat and gives the cat a small pouch to carry.

Once this is done, the cat takes to the woods and snares a rabbit. The cat then presents the rabbit to the king as a gift from the "Marquis of Carabus," a name the cat fabricated for his master. After a whirlwind of events involving an ogre and more gifts, the king is pleased enough to arrange a meeting between the cat's master and the king's beautiful daughter. The two fall in love and the king is delighted to give his blessing, believing the young man to be a generous nobleman. They live happily ever after and Puss in Boots retires from his hunting days to become a figure of great fame and importance. *Quel génie, ce chat!* He really was a genius

Les chats dans la langue française
- Cats in The French Language

Tales told by Mother Goose

French Nursery Rhymes

In French, nursery rhymes are called *comptines* or *chansons enfantines* (children's songs) and are a beloved part of French culture and history and form the basis of many cherished childhood memories. These *comptines* and *chansons enfantines* are used as teaching opportunities for learning about language to number skills, or even history and culture.

The "Mother Goose rhymes" in English are inspired by Charles Perrault's 1697 nursery rhyme collection *Contes de ma Mère l'Oye*. In the 20th century, Author Katherine Elwes-Thomas theorized that Mother Goose or Mère l'Oye might in turn be based on ancient legends of France's 10th century King Robert II's wife. Known as Berthe pied d'oie (Goose-Footed Bertha) or Berthe la fileuse (Bertha the Spinner), the French Queen was often described as spinning enrapturing tales for children.

Below is a French nursery rhyme (with English translation) all about a worried kitten who misses its "maman."

Mon Petit Chat	My Little Cat
-Miaou, miaou,	"Meow, meow!"
-Mon petit chat,	"My little cat,
Pourquoi es-tu si triste ?	Why are you so sad?"
-Miaou, miaou.	"Meow, meow!"
-Mon petit chat,	"My little cat,
Faut pas pleurer comme ça.	You mustn't cry like that."
-Ma maman est partie	"My mama went
Pour chasser les souris.	To hunt mice,
Tout seul dans mon panier,	All alone in my basket
Moi je m'ennuie.	I'm bored."

-Miaou, miaou !	"Meow, meow!"
-Mon petit chat,	"My little cat,
Pourquoi es-tu si triste ?	Why are you so sad?"
-Miaou, miaou !	"Meow, meow!"
-Mon petit chat,	"My little cat,
Faut pas pleurer comme ça.	You mustn't cry like that.
Ta maman reviendra,	Your mama will come back,
Elle te consolera,	She'll comfort you.
Au chaud dans ton panier,	In the warmth of your basket,
Tu rêveras.	You'll dream."

French Proverbs

What precisely is a proverb, you may ask? Compared to idioms or expressions, proverbs tend to offer some sort of advice, general truths or a philosophical idea in short and wise sayings. What's noteworthy about a proverb is that even translated from another language, it can convey its core message and be understood without further explanation or examination. Below are some feline-inspired proverbs from France:

"De beaux chats et un gros tas de fumier sont signes d'un bon fermier."

Literal Translation: Handsome cats and fat dung heaps are the sign of a good farmer

Meaning: A good farmer will be wise and invest in feeding his animals well, whether they provide pest control (mousers) or good food (through well-fertilized soil).

"Quand le chat n'est pas là, les souris dansent."

Literal Translation: When the cat is not there, the mice dance.

Meaning: This is the French equivalent of the English proverb "When the cat's away, the mice will play."

"Chat échaudé craint l'eau froide."

Literal Translation: A scalded cat fears cold water.

Meaning: This proverb signifies that someone who has had a bad experience with something will be wary of even similar, harmless situations. Once bitten, twice shy, in other words.

Kitty Idioms and Expressions

Every language has its own quirky turns of phrase, and French is no exception. Once the diplomatic language of European courts and aristocrats, French is rich with colorful expressions that don't always make sense when translated word for word. And unsurprisingly for a country so enamored with its feline companions, quite a few of these expressions feature cats. From mysterious metaphors to playful puns, these sayings reveal just how embedded cats are in the heart of French language and life. Below is an assortment of feline-related idioms and expressions:

- Appeler un chat un chat (calling a cat a cat) - saying things straight or as they are, without hesitation.

- Il n'y a pas un chat (there is not one cat around) – there is absolutely nobody there.

- Avoir un chat dans la gorge (to have a cat in the throat) - difficulty speaking caused by a sore throat

- C'est du pipi de chat (It's cat's pee) - it's nothing important

- Gourmande comme un chat (gourmand like a cat) - to be greedy but picky like a cat, won't settle for anything less than the best

Now you can go out there and impress the world with your newfound French sayings!

What French cats say

In French, a purr sound is called *ronron*, and cats *miaou* instead of meow. If a French cat is irritated, you might hear a hiss called a *feulement* or *sifflement*—both words used to describe a sharp, snake-like warning sound. Oh, là là! A cat's growl is called a *grognment*, just like a dog's growl, and kittens may let out an adorable *miaulement* when they want attention—yes, that's the noun form of *miauler*, "to meow." The act of purring, *ronronner*, is so well-regarded in France that the word *ronron-thérapie* exists—it refers to the calming, therapeutic benefits of a cat's purring. And don't forget the classic French baby talk for cats: instead of calling "Here, kitty kitty!", many French people say *Minou Minou*! or *P'tit chat!* (little cat!).

Le Jeu des Noms - The Name Game

Are you a francophile looking for the perfect French name for your cat? Finding the purr-fect name can be even tougher than naming your human newborn. The most common French names for cats are Minet (or Minette for females), Minou, Mistigri, Mimi, Felix, Tigrou (or Tigrette for females) …the list goes on! Did you know there's a special procedure for naming your pet in France? It's common practice to give your pet a name starting with a specific letter that changes every year. In 2018, for example, the letter was "O", and the top three French pet names of that year were Oslo, Oscar, and Olaf. Other fun names of that year were: Oreo, Olympe, Olli, Onyx, Olga, Oups (meaning Oopsy!), Opale, Owen, Opium, and Orion. In 2022, for example, the letter of the year was T, which means French cat owners could choose names like Topaze, Tigri or Timinou.

This name-giving tradition started in 1926 when the Société Centrale Canine, or Central Canine Society, made a rule that all dogs born in the same year would have a name that began with the same letter. The reason was because the society kept the names of certain dogs in a book called the LOF (Livre des origines Français) and that rule would keep the annual lists orderly. Eventually other pet owners, such as those who own cats, adopted this "rule." Not every letter is used, however, as "K," "Q," "W", "X," "Y," and "Z" are skipped over since it's more difficult to find names that begin with these letters.

Looking for something classy? Try Monsieur, Madame, Mademoiselle, Bijou (jewel), Chic, duchesse (like in Disney's 1970 film The Aristocats!), Pirouette (yes, like the ballet move), Velours (velvet), or Clochette (a small bell). Want something representative of your cat's generous proportions? Bouboule (fatty), Boulotte (big and short), Boulette (meatball), or Rondelet (chubby) might be just what you're looking for.

Les Cafés
-for people, and for cats!

Ready for a stroll through the streets of France? Embrace the spirit of the *flâneur*—a relaxed wanderer soaking up city life. And where is it better to pause than a café? Since the 18th century, cafés have been central to French culture, especially in Paris, where they've hosted debate, art, and conversation. By 2020, France had nearly 15,000 cafés, generating over 1.6 billion euros in sales—*très impressionnant!*

Coffee arrived in Paris in 1669 with Ottoman ambassador Suleiman Ağa and gained popularity in 1671 with an Armenian vendor named Pascal. The real breakthrough came in 1686 with Café Procope, a favorite of Enlightenment thinkers. Though coffee reached Versailles, it was hot chocolate that truly charmed Louis XIV. Later, coffee became the drink of choice for intellectuals. Voltaire reportedly drank dozens of tiny cups a day, often mixed with chocolate. Napoleon was a fan too, though claims of 50 daily cups are likely more legend than fact.

Cats have long been a fixture in French cafés, where they are often seen lazily hanging out on chairs or tables. In recent years, cat cafes have become popular in France, with several opening in major cities such as Paris and Lyon.

France's first cat café, Le Café des Chats, opened its doors in September 2013 and has been a hit with tourists and locals ever since. This popular destination for cat lovers was in a bourgeois district of Le Marais but relocated in 2016 to a second location that opened up in the more bohemian Bastille. No reservations are required to *regarder les chats*, but they are recommended due to the popularity of these kitties! The café permanently houses thirteen resident felines who are allowed to roam about freely in the shop except for the kitchen. All of the kitty residents were rescued from shelters, and a portion of Le Café des Chats's profits is donated to feline protection organizations.

In the 15th arrondissement of Paris, a quieter and less touristy part of the city is another cat café called Chat Mallows. This trendy café is decorated in pastels with plenty of obstacle courses and cozy boxes attached to the walls. Their resident felines have their own drink concoctions named after them in the shop's menu along with plenty of desserts. *Ronron!* –that's French for purr in case you didn't remember.

The Cats of France

If you are planning to visit some of these cat cafés, be aware that there are certain rules of etiquette to be followed. The cafés generally charge an admission fee that is by hour or visit and will require hand washing or sanitation before entrance. Some may even require you to remove your shoes or use slippers! Due to how busy it may get, your visits may be time limited. For the comfort of these lovely kitties, there can be rules to limit disturbing them, such as not picking up the cats, no disturbing the napping ones, and no flash photography. Honestly, I'd do anything to not disturb these lovely purrers in exchange for some calm companionship while indulging in good food and drink. *C'est le paradis*!

Philosophes et intellectuels - Philosophers and Intellectuals

The Cats of France

Jean-Jacques Rousseau

Now I have a confession, my kitty cat and I have a social contract. He knows he can do just about anything with no consequences as long as he gives me the look and a purr! Do you have something like that with your cat? Jean-Jacques Rousseau, though born in French-speaking Geneva in 1712, became a central figure in French Enlightenment thought developing the key concept of a social contract to describe the implicit agreement between a country's government and its citizens. His political philosophy—especially in works like the aforementioned *The Social Contract,* and the *Discourse on Inequality* helped shape the era's ideals and later influenced aspects of the French Revolution. In these texts, Rousseau argued that government should serve the common good and protect the rights and freedoms of its citizens rather than autocratically rule over them as monarchs had in the past. Rousseau was also fond of cats, associating their independence with human liberty. In a 1764 conversation with English biographer and diarist James Boswell, Rousseau asked, "Do you like cats?" When Boswell replied that he didn't, Rousseau responded, "I was sure of that. It is my test of character... Men do not like cats because the cat is free and will never consent to become a slave." He continued, "A hen would obey your orders if you could make her understand them, but a cat will understand you perfectly and not obey them." This view of cats as free-spirited and resistant to domination echoed in later centuries. While cats were long linked with superstition, by the early 20th century, particularly through anarchist and labor movements like the Industrial Workers of the World, the black cat had become a symbol of wildcat strikes and rebellion against authority.

Jacques Derrida

What do you think cats think about when they give you the stare? You must know what I'm talking about. Well, one French cat lover had some interesting observations on that topic.

French-Algerian philosopher Jacques Derrida was born in 1930 in El Biar, a suburb of Algiers, in what was then French Algeria. He is best known for developing an approach known as deconstruction, a critical method that analyzes the relationship between text, meaning, and interpretation. Deconstruction challenges the idea that texts have fixed, stable meanings by highlighting the inherent ambiguities, contradictions, and assumptions within language. Derrida's work had a major impact on philosophy, literature, and critical theory, and it significantly influenced the humanities and social sciences, particularly in fields like literary theory, linguistics, psychoanalysis, and cultural studies.

In his work *The Animal That Therefore I Am,* published in 2002, Derrida discusses the intricacies of animals versus humans. More notably, he focuses on the discomfort when he notices his own cat, staring at his naked form. Do your animals give you an awkward stare? Can you relate to the heebie-jeebies that come from their excruciating stare-down? Derrida writes about his sense of discomfort and even shame of being naked in the presence of his cat's gaze. It breaks the categorizing of the cat as just an "animal." Normally humans are the "observers" with the privilege of examining, naming, and judging what we see but Derrida noticed some philosophical insight in seeing his cat, with its own individualistic sentience, as being the examiner.

La Musique
- Music and the Purr-Forming Arts

Feline Melodies

We've detailed elsewhere (under the Major French Cat Lovers section of this book) the story of wealthy 17th-century harpist Madame Dupuis, who reportedly loved her cultured cats so much that their care became the main focus of her will and testament but she was far from the only French musician to have a such a feline connection. Moving to the 19th century, Polish composer Frédéric Chopin was romantically involved with French novelist George Sand (the masculine pen name of Aurore Lucile Dupin). During their time together, they lived in Nohant, about 240km south of Paris and cats were an integral part of the household. While there is no concrete evidence that Chopin was directly inspired by cats in his compositions, a popular anecdote claims that his "Minute Waltz" (Waltz in D-flat major, Op. 64, No. 1) was inspired by a cat running across the piano keys.

French composer Claude Debussy, born in 1862, was indeed a cat lover. He often allowed his feline companions to roam freely in his workspace and affectionately described how they would "sow disorder among the pencils"—a charming metaphor for their creative interference. In the 20th century, Colette—a renowned French author—and Maurice Ravel, composer of Boléro, both adored cats. Colette wrote extensively about them, turning her own pets into literary characters. Ravel, who had two beloved Siamese cats, often mentioned them in letters and was known to sign off with playful feline farewells like "Je te lèche le bout du nez" ("I lick the tip of your nose"). The two collaborated on the opéra-féerie (fairytale opera) *L'Enfant et les Sortilèges* (The Child and the Spells), which premiered in 1925 with a libretto by Colette and music by Ravel. The opera tells the story of a misbehaving boy who torments animals, objects, and nature, only for these beings to come to life and teach him a lesson. Among them are a male and female cat who appear in the flirtatious *Duo miaulé* ("Meowed Duet"), a scene in which they rub against each other, moan, and meow in an operatic parody of romantic passion—one of the most memorable and whimsical moments in the piece.

Le cinéma
- French Feline Movie Stars

Film Pioneers with Paws

The French played a pioneering role in the birth of cinema, beginning with the Lumière brothers' invention of the cinématographe in 1895. This device was the first practical motion picture camera and projector, capable of recording, developing, and projecting moving images onto a screen for a large audience. Given France's foundational role in cinema, it's no surprise that French culture not only cherishes the art of filmmaking but also views cinema as a vital part of societal dialogue and a mirror of its history and identity. And yes, cats did appear in some of the earliest French films...

Long before cats took over the internet, they had already made their mark in the pioneering days of French science and cinema. In 1887, famed physiologist Étienne-Jules Marey captured the elegant motion of a cat transitioning from a trot to a gallop using his groundbreaking chronophotographic camera. This was more than a scientific curiosity—it was part of Marey's broader effort to understand the mechanics of movement, contributing foundational insights to both biomechanics and early motion picture technology.

A few years later, around 1896, early film pioneers such as the Lumière brothers embraced a more whimsical approach with *Le Déjeuner du chat* ("The Cat's Lunch"), a brief one-shot film that shows a cat sitting at a table, daintily enjoying a meal—just like a proper Parisian diner.

Gay Purr-ee

Ever have big dreams to run away to a big city? Maybe someplace romantic like Paris? Mewsette, the leading kitty of American animated musical film Gay Purr-ee made her dream a reality. Produced by United Productions of America and released by Warner Bros. in 1962, Gay Purr-ee stars Judy Garland as the voice of Mewsette in her only animated film role and Robert Goulet as the voice of love interest Jaune-Tom in his very first feature film.

Set in 1895 France, bushy-tailed Angora Mewsette is bored with her simple farm life in rural Provence in southeastern France. She is so inspired by stories of glamorous and sophisticated Paris that she leaves her "clumsy country clod" love, Jaune-Tom, to hop a train to the big city where she meets con artist cat Meowrice. He takes advantage of her country cat naïveté and tricks her into believing he and Madame Henrietta Reubens-Chatte will turn her into "The Belle of all Paris." Instead, Mewsette is groomed to be a mail-order bride to a rich fat-cat, Mr. Henry Phtt in Pittsburg. Meanwhile, Jaune-Tom and his friend Robespierre get into various antics as they try to find Mewsette, including getting sent to Alaska. Luckily, they return to France and find Mewsette just before she is shipped off to the US. All three manage to escape Meowrice, who they send to Pittsburg instead, and they live happily ever after in Paris. Ah, to live la vie en rose of young lovers!

Le Chat

It's not difficult to fall in love with a cat but what about being jealous of said cat? This is the situation explored in 1971's French drama film *Le Chat* directed by Pierre Granier-Deferre. Based on a 1967 novel by Georges Simenon, it follows an elderly married couple with a complicated relationship. After 25 years of marriage, they've grown tired of each other and developed mutual mistrust. The film became one of cinema's bleakest commentaries on married life.

As the film's plot unfolds, the once loving and passionate husband Julien, played by Jean Gabin, now only shows affection to a stray cat, Greffier. The wife Clemence, played by Simone Signoret, is irritated by the cat receiving attention as it represents everything she wants to revive in their marriage. Eventually this leads to an understanding that the couple cannot live without one another, but they also cannot continue inflicting pain on each other. The film's tagline upon release sums it up as: "A love-hate relationship so strong it destroyed everything — the man, the woman, — even the cat."

A Musical Cat Lover

Chat Écoutant la Musique (Cat Listening to Music) is a 1988 short film directed by the renowned French filmmaker Chris Marker. With a runtime of approximately three minutes, this documentary features Marker's own cat, Guillaume-en-Egypte, as he listens to a piece of piano music. In *Chat Écoutant la Musique*, the camera captures Guillaume-en-Egypte sprawled across a Yamaha DX7 keyboard, seemingly entranced by the delicate notes of Federico Mompou's Pájaro Triste. The cat's subtle movements—twitching ears, gentle stretches, and occasional glances—mirror the music's ebb and flow, creating a serene and intimate portrait of feline contentment. The film's minimalist approach and focus on a quiet, contemplative moment highlights the appreciation for music that cats and humans share.

A Cat in Paris

We can all agree that cats are incredibly cunning, right? This is especially true with Dino, the cat living a double life in *A Cat in Paris*. Known in France as Une vie de chat is a 2010 animated adventure crime film created by Folimage, a French 2D animation studio, and directed by Alain Gagnol and Jean-Loup Felicioli. The film received highly positive reviews and was nominated for an Academy Award for Best Animated Feature.

The story follows a little Parisian girl as she unravels a thrilling mystery with the help of her cat, Dino. The black cat with a small white patch actually lives a double life. At night he is Mr. Cat who follows a burglar named Nico performing jewel heists, but by day he is simply Dino the housecat who lives a quiet life with a mute girl named Zoé. One evening, upon following Dino outside, Zoé encounters a thieving gang connected with her father's death. She is spotted and the gang begins to pursue her. After much miscommunication and unfortunate happenings, burglar Nico, loyal cat Dino, and Zoé's police superintendent mother Jeanne come to her rescue. Happily, the film ends with the heroine Zoé regaining her voice, the burglar Nico reforming his ways as well as becoming a part of her family, and Dino, the former detective's helper retiring to be a pampered full-time house pet.

Le Science
-Scientific Kitties

Solid or Liquid?

Have you seen your cat in action as it squeezes in places it shouldn't be able to or plop down and fill your bathroom sink with itself? Have you ever wondered if a cat can be simultaneously both solid and a liquid? A French physics researcher by the name of Marc-Antoine Fardin of the Université Paris Diderot did wonder just that in his science paper questioning: "Can a Cat Be Both a Solid and a Liquid?"

Fardin concluded that cats "who are known to be solid most of the time, can be classified as liquid under certain circumstances." Since a cat can "relax" or deform into a state that takes up the shape of a container without a change in volume, a kitty can apparently be classified as a liquid! How cool is that? In 2017, Fardin received an Ig Nobel for physics for his great work! The Ig Nobel Prizes are awarded for scientific research that makes people laugh, then think. These are serious (and often quite inventive) studies that address unusual or humorous questions.

A Cat's Fall

"The expression of offended dignity shown by the cat at the end of the first series indicates a want of interest in scientific investigation." — Marey in *Nature*, 1894

In 1894, French physiologist and motion photography pioneer Étienne-Jules Marey captured a now-famous sequence of images of a cat falling midair to study the feline righting reflex. Using his chronophotographic camera (which could take up to 12 images per second), Marey demonstrated that cats are able to reorient themselves in free fall without any external pivot point — contradicting the belief that the cat used the person's hand as a fulcrum. Instead, Marey's study revealed that cats twist their bodies using internal angular momentum, beginning with a rotation of the front half of the body, followed by the rear. Marey published his findings in *Comptes Rendus* with an English summary in Nature, where the editors noted, with dry humor, the cat's "expression of offended dignity" at being so unceremoniously observed.

Although often mistakenly labeled a film, Marey's "falling cat" sequence was not a Lumière production and not a cinematic motion picture, but rather a series of still images — a crucial step in the evolution of motion analysis and one of the earliest visual studies of animal biomechanics.

Cats and Communication

In 2023 French researchers Charlotte de Mouzon and Gérard Leboucher of the Université Paris Nanterre set out to unravel the mysteries of feline etiquette—specifically, how French cats prefer to be approached by unfamiliar humans. They conducted their research on quiet mornings in cat cafés in Bordeaux and Toulouse, observing cats in a dozen café cats to see which forms of communication—vocal, visual, or both, attracted the cats.

Ever notice that your cat ignores your calls but responds when you make eye contact or offer a hand, like a Parisian maître d' inviting you to your table? The French researchers found cats are much more responsive to visual cues, such as extending a hand or giving a slow, gentle blink-than to the classic French "pff pff" cat call or simply calling their name. In the study, ten out of twelve cats approached when greeted visually, compared to only seven for vocal calls alone. When both visual and vocal cues were combined, eleven cats responded.

What does this mean for cat owners, whether they are in Lyon, Lille, or Los Angeles? If you want your cat's attention, don't just rely on your voice. Channel your inner Parisian: use expressive gestures, offer your hand, and try the famous slow blink. Cats are tuned in to your body language and facial expressions, not just your words. This approach not only makes your cat feel more at ease—less an indignant *sacré bleu*! and more *pas de problème*—but can also strengthen the bond between you. So, next time you want your cat to come to you, skip the shouting and try a subtle gesture or a soft, knowing blink. With a little knowledge from those French cat communication experts, you might just find your cat is far more attentive—and a little less aloof—than you imagined.

Les grandes odyssées felines -Feline Explorers and Adventurers

Former stray Félicette who was sent into space in 1963 by French researchers.

The Cats of France

Félicette, the first (and only) cat in space

The French Space Program is the third oldest, established just after the American and Soviet space programs. However, there were allusions to the concepts of space travel and rocketry in French culture long before the technological means were available. French novelist Jules Gabriel Verne wrote *From the Earth to the Moon* in 1865 and George Méliès created the well-known 1902 film *A Trip to the Moon*. Given how space travel captured the French imagination, it's hardly surprising that France was also the first and only nation to send a cat into the cosmos. Félicette is the only cat to have been launched into space, and she returned alive! She was originally given the rather dull, but scientific name of C 341 before the flight and was 1 of 14 female cats that were being trained for space flight over the course of two months. The cats had electrodes implanted into their skulls for study and monitoring while electrical impulses were sent to the brain and leg for stimulated responses. The media, upon receiving her biological data, decided this history-making cat needed a more appealing name and starting calling C 341 "Félix" after the cartoon series Félix the Cat before they knew her gender. When they realized, the cat was "une femme," her name was changed from the masculine "Felix" to the feminine version and adopted officially as "Félicette" by the French space research agency, CERMA.

Other animals in space preceded Felicette the French cat's space flight. Fruit flies were the first humble astronauts sent by the US in the late 1940s. In 1949, the US sent the first mammal into space, a Rhesus monkey named Albert II. In 1957, the Soviet Union launched Laika, a stray dog, into space aboard Sputnik II. France became the third country to launch animals into space with the sending of Hector the rat in February 1961 from France's base in the Sahara. France then chose cats as the next animal for space flight as they wanted a larger mammal and they already had a large amount of neurological data on cats.

On the 18th of October 1963, Felicette, who had been chosen for her calm demeanor, was launched into space from the CERMA site in Algeria. The suborbital flight lasted 13 minutes and she was subjected to 5 minutes of weightlessness in which her heart rate slowed and breathing was nominal. Felicette was then recovered safely by helicopter after the vessel she was traveling in landed upside down in the sea. The mission made her the very first cat to successfully reach space— and the only cat since.

The mission was a large milestone for France and helped bring the country into the space race. Félicette has been commemorated in stamps by former French colonies, had a "Pays D'oc Grenache Rouge" wine named after her (how very French!) and in 2019 received a bronze statue honoring her contribution to science. This sculpture to commemorate Felicette was crowdfunded by a Kickstarter campaign set up by Matthew Serge Guy in 2017. Designed by sculptor Gill Parker, the statue of Félicette gazing at the sky while sitting on our beautiful blue planet is at the International Space University in Strasbourg, France.

Misele

Farm cat Misele was so devoted to her owner 82-year-old Alfonse Mondry that she couldn't be apart from him when he had to be taken to a hospital nine miles away in Sarrebourg, in the northeast of France. The poor kitty must have crossed many fields, rock quarries, bridges, forests, and busy highways but she made her way to the hospital that she had never been to before. She even found his room! She was allowed to stay after the nurses found her that evening happily purring away in the lap of her owner.

Cocci

Laëtitia de Amicis and her family moved from their family home in the Orne region of France along with their three cats to a new location in Normandy. Somehow, one of the cats named Cocci disappeared in August 2021. For three months the family continued looking with no luck and Laëtitia told her children Cocci may have gone back home in Orne to look for them, not believing herself that it could be true.

Then Laëtitia saw a Facebook post about a cat found just five miles away from their previous home and immediately recognized the cat as their very own Coci. Laëtitia had her dad go identify the cat. He was reluctant to believe the same cat had actually travelled the country, more than 280 miles, to get to their old family home. However, the cat only answered to Cocci and a vet confirmed the cat was 10 years old and spayed, just like Cocci! As soon as the rest of the family went to retrieve her, Cocci recognized them instantly. She ended up staying at the vet for three weeks recuperating from the injuries she had sustained during her time as a stray. Once home she adapted very quickly and made up for all the lost cuddling time!

The Hatching Cat

In the early 20th century the French had their very own celebrity cat. The French Hatching Cat was a large fluffy Angora who mothered—you guessed it! Baby chicks! This Angora hailed from Paris where she enjoyed sitting on eggs and being surrounded by the adopted baby chicks that she helped hatch.

The cat was so well-loved and gained such international fame that she journeyed outside France to New York City in June of 1911 and crossed the Hudson River to the Palisades Amusement Park in New Jersey. There, the mothering kitty spent six weeks showing off her nurturing skills. She was quite popular and many amusement park owners wanted her to grace their venues and Nick Shenk, the owner of the Palisades Amusement Park had to outbid other American amusement park owners for the right to display this famous kitty. This wasn't just some random circus act either, the famous feline travelled under the special care of Fernand Akoud, the ethnological departments director of the Jardin d'Acclimation or the Zoological Gardens in Paris.

Les chats dans les arts visuels
-Cats in the Visual Arts

Artists who Loved Cats

"A little drowsing cat is an image of perfect beatitude."

—Jules Champfleury (1820–1889), French art critic and cat appreciator

In France, art is practically a national pastime—somewhat like philosophizing over a café crème. And where there is French art, there are often French cats: lounging, judging, occasionally knocking over a carefully arranged bowl of fruit. From medieval tapestries to Montmartre ateliers, cats have slipped into the brushstrokes and margins of French culture with the nonchalance only they can pull off.

While Italy may have sparked the Renaissance, it was France that turned the artist's studio into a salon—and in many cases, a cat sanctuary. Whether sprawled across a chaise longue in a Rococo daydream or prowling through a Post-Impressionist still life, cats made themselves at home in the nation's visual imagination. After all, who better understands the moodiness of Romanticism or the aloof brilliance of Surrealism than a cat?

French artists, ever attuned to mystery and mischief, found in their feline companions a kind of furry muse: elegant yet unpredictable, aloof yet omnipresent. What follows is a curated selection through some cats as French artists saw them and captured them for immortality.

We begin in 1747 with *Magdaleine Pinceloup de la Grange, née de Parseval*, a portrait by Jean-Baptiste Perronneau. Here, the sitter's calm and composed demeanor is complemented by the presence of a domestic cat, a rare inclusion in formal portraiture of the era. This painting signals the growing sentimental value of pets among the French elite, and the association of cats with refined, if slightly mysterious, femininity.

Séamus Mullarkey

Magdaleine Pinceloup de la Grange, née de Parseval by Jean-Baptiste Perronneau
1747

Jumping ahead to 1775, Marguerite Gérard's Le déjeuner du chat (The Cat's Lunch) paints an intimate bourgeois scene where a cat is not just a passive background detail, but an active participant. Gérard, one of the few prominent female artists of the time, injects the work with gentle humor and warm domesticity, capturing the social elevation of cats from barn companions to pampered housemates.

The Cats of France

Le déjeuner du chat (The Cat's Lunch) by French painter Marguerite Gérard, 1775

Around the turn of the 19th century, Jean-Jacques Bachelier's Un Chat Angola showcases the exotic appeal of the Angora breed—a long-haired, elegant feline. Bachelier, who often painted animals and was deeply interested in naturalism, presents the cat with almost scientific exactness, while still celebrating its beauty.

Un Chat Angola by French painter Jean-Jacques Bachelier

By the mid-19th century, cats had fully secured their place in French households, as shown in *Chatte et ses petits* (Cat and Her Kittens) by Octavie Rossignon. Painted circa 1850, the scene offers a tender glimpse of feline maternity. Rossignon elevates the cat to a symbol of nurturing calm, emphasizing its capacity for gentleness and domestic grace—values deeply cherished in the era's artistic and moral outlook.

The Cats of France

Chatte et ses petits (Cat and Her Kittens) by Octavie Rossignon 19th century

In 1868, Édouard Manet—one of the great disruptors of the art world—surprised many with *The Cats' Rendezvous*, a work that tempers his typical radicalism with a touch of whimsy. Known for his bold depictions of Parisian life, controversial nudes, and a sharp eye for social commentary, Manet here turns his gaze to something quite different The scene is playful, even theatrical, with anthropomorphized felines engaging in a nocturnal tryst.

Manet's interest in cats wasn't just artistic. He owned a cat named Zizi, who lived with him and his wife Suzanne Leenhoff. Zizi, a white or light-colored feline, appears in some of Manet's more intimate paintings, such as *Woman with a Cat* (1880), where she curls up contentedly in Suzanne's lap. Friends and correspondents recalled Manet's habit of including little watercolor doodles of cats in his letters—tiny, affectionate gestures that revealed a lighter, playful side to the often serious, melancholic painter. It seems that for Manet, cats were more than just studio props. They were companions, muses, and occasional stand-ins for human character—aloof yet curious, elegant yet defiant. Just like his art.

Séamus Mullarkey

LE RENDEZ-VOUS DES CHATS

Sketch based *on Manet's The Cats' Rendezvous* 1868

In the 1870s and 1880s, Jules Gustave Leroy became known for his charming and humorous depictions of cats, often shown in playful and mischievous poses. His works—frequently given informal titles such as *Playful Cats* or *Time to Play*—exude a sense of cats' affectionate and silly side. Leroy's brush danced as much as his subjects did, capturing feline liveliness with a joyful spirit that endeared him to an ever-increasing audience of cat lovers.

Time to Play by Jules Gustave Leroy, oil on canvas

Playful Cats by French painter Jules Leroy, born in 1856.

During the same period, Pierre-Auguste Renoir contributed significantly to the Impressionist canon of cat imagery. His *Woman with a Cat* (c. 1875–1880) features a serene feline cradled in the arms of a softly rendered woman, blending sensuality with tranquility. In 1887, Renoir painted *La petite fille au chat,* a touching portrait of young Julie Manet, daughter of Berthe Morisot. The cat in her arms is more than a pet—it's a companion in innocence, emblematic of the tender emotional bonds that Impressionists so often celebrated. In other works like *Boy with Cat* (Claude Renoir) and *Sleeping Girl with Cat*, felines appear nestled in laps, lounging on cushions, or basking in domestic

The Cats of France

warmth. For Renoir, cats were not background detail but expressive symbols of softness and the joys of everyday life.

La petite fille au chat (Young Girl with a Cat) - a portrait of Julie Manet with her cat by Renoir

Séamus Mullarkey

French Impressionist artist Pierre Auguste Renoir's *Woman with a Cat* (1875)

Finally, the end of the 19th century—the fin-de-siècle era—brings us to *Des Chats* (1898) by Théophile Steinlen, the undisputed master of Parisian cats. Best known for his iconic 1896 poster *Tournée du Chat Noir*, which advertised the bohemian Montmartre cabaret and helped cement the cat as a symbol of avant-garde Paris, Steinlen brought the same sensibility to *Des Chats*. In this richly illustrated portfolio of twenty-eight illustrations, cats appear in all facets of daily life—lounging on windowsills, stalking through alleyways, or curled beside children—

rendered with stylized lines and expressive energy. Part symbol, part satire, part celebration, the images function not only as artistic studies but as cultural declarations: cats belong on posters, in paintings, and in the public imagination.

Cover of *Des Chats* by Théophile Steinlen 1898

La céramique - Ceramics

Émile Gallé's green pottery cat circa 1895

The Cats of France

French artist and major innovator in the French Art Nouveau movement Émile Gallé is known for his glasswork and furniture, but he is also known for his many Gallé cats. In the late 1800s, he made quite a few of these smiling pottery cats, in colors like green or yellow, adorned with blue hearts, from his ceramics factory in Nancy, France. It became a popular design style and similar looking cat statues were made in other countries. Although copies, these cats are also sometimes called "Gallé Cats" even if not made by Gallé himself. These fun and popular cats are still being collected today. Don't you want one of the original Gallé cats to sit in your living room? Well, you might want to dig deep in your wallet. A recent auction sold one of his cats for £4,000 or about $5,000!

Des armoiries à la publicité -From Coats of Arms to Advertising

Nestlé's Swiss Milk - Richest in Cream, poster by Théophile Steinlen

The Cats of France

Although they say not to judge a book by its cover— I'd unashamedly be interested in anything with a cute cat on it, wouldn't you? It wasn't always memes about wanting cheezburgers or advertising, cat imagery can be found way back to the Middle Ages. Even though the cat was sometimes poorly regarded by the Christian Church for being possibly aligned with witchcraft, the domestic cat sometimes found itself in heraldry, the visual representation of aristocratic families. It was more common for larger cats like lions or leopards to be represented in noble imagery due to the stigma, but some families like the Chetaldie family of Limoges, France carried two domestic argent (silver or white) cats on an azure blue shield as their coat-of-arms. In about the fifth to sixth century, St. Clotilda, daughter of Chilperic the Burgundy King, and wife of the King of Franks, Clovis, had a cat sable (with dark fur) on her armorial bearings. It was shown fiercely pouncing on a rat!

The equalizing of classes that came with the French Revolution saw the abolition of noble titles. This also meant that family coat-of-arms were basically abolished, including those that had included kitty cat imagery. However, cats continued to be used to advertise the names of shops such as "The Fishing Cat" shop which sold fish tackle. The road the long-closed shop used to sit on is now named "Rue du Chat-qui-Pêche" or "Street of the Fishing Cat." If you want to take a walk down this narrow thoroughfare it can be found in Paris, on the Left Bank.

Cat lover Théophile Steinlen created Paris's most famous and commercially reproduced cat in his Le Chat Noir poster advertising the cabaret of the same name. Le Chat Noir was a popular hangout for avant garde artists, writers, musicians and more in bohemian Montmartre of the 1880s-90s. Even after the cabaret's closing in 1897, Steinlen's lithograph black cat poster lived on and grew even more famous. Steinlen also had a personal affection for cats and was known to feed dozens of local kitties in Montmartre, a northern district on the right bank of Paris where French artists found community for centuries

At the time, cats were symbolic of bohemia. Le Chat Noir nightclub was frequented by musicians, poets, artists, and the working-class of Paris. This mélange of classes discussed workers' rights and philosophy new and unusual *avant garde* ideas. In France mages of black cats came to symbolize artistic freedom and represent art-nouveau, the New Art movement at the fin-de-siècle, the end of the 19th century.

Aside from advertising cabarets, cats have been used to advertise consumer goods. In 1915, the Gold Starry company of Paris who produced the first fountain pens created a cat-centric advertising strategy. The Art Nouveau styled advert features a beautiful white cat writing with a Gold Starry fountain pen saying, "I no longer write like a cat." Get it? It refers to a common French expression stating that bad writing is like that "of a cat." Some in the US might refer to such handwritten scrawl as "chicken scratch." Steinlen also created a beloved poster for Nestlé's Swiss Milk—showing his daughter, Colette, drinking from a bowl while curious cats surround her. Meanwhile, one of the most iconic absinthe advertisements of the Belle Époque, the Absinthe Bourgeois poster (c. 1900–1902) by the Mourgue Brothers, features a sleek black cat savoring absinthe, the controversially dangerous anise liqueur. Even today, Parisian shops like the bookstore Le Dilettante continue in the tradition of feline marketing: its logo—a black cat sleeping atop an open book—demonstrates how cats still carry alluring selling power.

Très bizarre!-Very Strange

Postcard image of Louis Coulon and his 11ft beard as a nest for a cat.
1890

Louis Coulon and his cuddly beard

This remarkable heavily bearded man was a skilled iron caster, making molds for ironworks. He was born in the Montluçon commune in central France in 1826. By the age of twelve, Louis Coulon was supposedly already shaving at such a frequency that he couldn't keep a sharp edge on his razor blade. By the age of fourteen, the length of his beard was almost twenty inches! In later years it was supposed to have reached eleven feet. Not surprisingly, due to his odd physical quirk, Coulon became rather famous and his image soon adorned postcards, newspapers, and magazines. Apparently, Coulon must have been quite the cat lover, as quite a few images depict kitties cozily nested in his beard. Those savvy felines are always on the lookout for somewhere to take a comfy nap!

Cats in the Night Sky

In 1799, French astronomer Joseph Jérôme de Lalande—an ardent cat lover—introduced the constellation Felis ("the Cat"), making up we suppose for the lack of feline representation in the heavens. He collaborated with Johann Bode to include the kitty-themed constellation in Bode's 1801 *Uranographia*. Despite its inclusion in many 19th-century atlases, the Felis constellation was ultimately dropped when the International Astronomical Union formalized the 88 modern constellations in the 1920s and 1930s. Interestingly, in 2018, the IAU honored cats by bestowing the name Felis on the star HD 85951. Meanwhile, the sky retains three dog-themed constellations, but no official constellation based on a domestic cat—an astronomical slight that should be rectified I feel.

Le Futur
-The Future for French Cats

"Juste les Essentiels, Madame" -The Facts, Ma'am, Just the Facts

Did you know?

- France has the highest number of cats in Europe!

- **Cats win over dogs as pets in France** - French cats numbered 15.1 million in 2021 while there were only 7.5 million dogs in the country. This is most likely due to cats, with their relative ease of care, being a better fit for the modern French lifestyle. Their sheer numbers mean that cats dominate the French pet food market and market trends see that dominance growing as more and more households fall under the feline spell!

- **The foods of the future** - The growth in French cat parents is attributed to two factors: an ever-ageing population with an increasing number of pensioners and a steady decline in birth rates in the nation. An aging population would apparently find cats a better pet as they don't need energetic walks as dogs would. Fewer human babies may be leading to a greater emphasis on little fur babies, like kitties. For both of these reasons, felines have succeeded in becoming true members of the new nuclear French family and as they do so, French pet parents are more focused on their health and their diet, leaning towards more natural and organic products. This drives the market to focusing on developing healthier and more nutritionally sound foods. Major French cat food companies are investing in the research and development of new products and variations on current products. There is also a focus on launching new products at lower prices. Current top pet food market leaders in France are Mars, Inc (including Royal Canin), Hill's Pet Nutrition, Inc., United Petfood, Diamond Petfood, and Nestlé SA (Purina).

A New French Sub-Species: The Cat-Fox

The locals on the French island of Corsica have long referred in the regional language to a "ghjattu volpe" or "cat-fox." Is it a cat or is it a fox? *Qu'est-ce que c'est?* These creatures are nocturnal hunters that look more cat than fox but are bigger than a regular house cat with large, ringed tails and extremely sharp canine teeth like a fox. In 2012, scientists studied the "cat-fox" DNA from fur left on an affectionately loved-on stick that was coated in an attractant scent. Studying the DNA established that the creature is different from the *Felis silvestris silvestris* European wildcat and is in fact closer to the DNA of the *Felis silvestris lybica* African wildcat. The Agence France-Presse (AFP) said in 2019 that researchers believe the feline may have been brought to Corsica by farmers around 6500 B.C.

In 2023, after further genetic testing, the French office for Biodiversity (OFB) finally announced that the "cat-fox" is its own unique subspecies of wild cat specific to the island. This discovery is a step towards ensuring these unique wild cats can be properly protected in the future. They stated that the "cat-foxes" have their own special genetic strain and can be clearly distinguished from any other wild or domestic cat. The creature measures 90 cm or 35 inches from head to tail. The tail is distinct in its rings and black tip. It has wide ears, short whiskers, and fox-like canine teeth. There are stripes on its front legs, darker hind legs, and it has a red-brown tummy. Its dense, silky fur may offer natural resistance to parasites such as fleas, ticks, and lice—an adaptation that could have helped it thrive in the Corsican wilderness.

Moving to France with Your Cat

The Cats of France

If you decide to up sticks and move to France with your fur companion, France welcomes pets. However, moving with a pet, especially internationally, can be a tough journey with strict rules and regulations to follow.

Here are some tips for your and your cat's move:

- Always be sure you have the correct papers and forms that France requires for pets from your country (as well as appropriate documentation for any countries you might pass through on your way to France).

- Pets within Europe can take advantage of European Pet Passports. Designed for domestic animals as a certification of health, they are issued by a licensed vet. The ID will contain an identification number, proof of vaccinations and any other essential information for your pet's travels. It is also valid for the entire life of your pet!

- Be sure your pet is microchipped and up to date on vaccinations. If your pet is coming to France from a country with a high incidence of rabies, your pet must have a Blood Titer Test for rabies one month after vaccination and three months prior to departure. So, be sure to plan if necessary.

Happy travels! Bon voyage!

En guise de conclusion…
-By means of conclusion…

As we conclude our journey through the enchanting world of France's feline inhabitants, it becomes evident that these cats are more than mere companions; they are integral to the culture and history of the nation. From the cobblestone streets of Paris to the tranquil countryside of Provence, cats have left their indelible paw prints on French art, literature, and daily life.

Throughout this book, we have explored the diverse roles cats have played in French life—from the mystical witches' companions of olden times to the cherished pets of literary giants. Cats, with their unique personalities and intriguing stories, have not only inspired but also comforted and entertained countless French people across generations.

In closing, let us not forget the lessons these cats impart: the importance of curiosity, the value of independence, and the beauty of living in the moment. Whether lounging in a sunbeam or chasing after the wind, the cats of France invite us to embrace life with a sense of wonder and appreciation for the world around us.

Thank you for embarking on this journey with me. May the stories and images of these magnificent cats stay with you, bringing a touch of French elegance and feline charm into your own life.

L'auteur
-About the Author-
-Séamus Mullarkey...

I am a cat fanatic and book lover; I write fascinating books about our beloved kitties and how they've shaped our world.

— If you love cats, you'll love my books —

So, why not join my *"Cats of the World"* fan club? You can read all my new books FOR FREE!

AND... You'll get a free bonus book, *"How to Speak French With Your Cat"*...

SIMPLY SCAN THE CODE OR CLICK THE LINK TO JOIN!
There's no cost to you
subscribepage.io/7565d5

More From Seamus Mullarkey

Would you like to read more of my books???

Just click or scan below…

SCAN TO VIEW DETAILS…

More From Seamus Mullarkey

Would you like to read more of my books???

Just click or scan below…

SCAN TO VIEW DETAILS…

More From Seamus Mullarkey

Would you like to read more of my books???

Just click or scan below...

SCAN TO VIEW DETAILS...

More From Seamus Mullarkey

Would you like to read more of my books???

Just click or scan below…

SCAN TO VIEW DETAILS…

DON'T MISS THIS SPECIAL BONUS

GET YOUR *FREE BOOK* TODAY

IT'S SO SIMPLE – AND TOTALLY FREE! – SCAN THE CODE OR CLICK THE LINK....

subscribepage.io/7565d5

Please leave a review...

If this book brought you a few moments of pleasure, I'd be so grateful if you took just a few moments to leave a review on the book's Amazon page.

You can get to the review page with the QR code below. Thanks!

Purrr-leeze leave a review!

s'il vous plaît...

www.ingramcontent.com/pod-product-compliance
Lightning Source LLC
LaVergne TN
LVHW011427080426
835512LV00005B/300